W9-AJP-744

J
523
mor

Learning About the Sun, Moon, Planets, and Stars

WORLD BOOK

a Scott Fetzer company

Chicago

www.worldbookonline.com

World Book, Inc.
233 N. Michigan Avenue
Chicago, IL 60601
U.S.A.

For information about other World Book publications,
visit our website at **http://www.worldbookonline.com**
or call **1-800-WORLDBK (967-5325)**.

For information about sales to schools and libraries, call
1-800-975-3250 (United States);
1-800-837-5365 (Canada).

Library of Congress Cataloging-in-Publication Data

Learning about the sun, moon, planets, and stars.
    p. cm. -- (Learning playground)
  Includes index.
  Summary: "An activity-based volume that introduces
early-level astronomy concepts, including the sun, moon,
stars, and planets in our solar system. Features include a
glossary, an additional resource list, and an index"--
Provided by publisher.
  ISBN 978-0-7166-0232-3
  1. Astronomy--Juvenile literature. I. World Book, Inc.
  QB46.L43 2011
  523--dc22
                        2011004732

STAFF

Executive Committee
President: Donald D. Keller
Vice President and
  Editor in Chief: Paul A. Kobasa
Vice President, Marketing/
  Digital Products: Sean Klunder
Vice President, International: Richard Flower
Director, Human Resources: Bev Ecker

Editorial
Associate Manager, Supplementary
  Publications: Cassie Mayer
Editor: Mike DuRoss
Researcher: Annie Brodsky
Manager, Contracts & Compliance
  (Rights & Permissions): Loranne K. Shields
Indexer: David Pofelski

Graphics and Design
Manager: Tom Evans
Coordinator, Design Development and
  Production: Brenda B. Tropinski
Senior Designer: Isaiah Sheppard
Associate Designer: Matt Carrington
Photographs Editor: Clover Morell

Pre-Press and Manufacturing
Director: Carma Fazio
Manufacturing Manager: Barbara Podczerwinski
Production/Technology Manager:
  Anne Fritzinger

Learning Playground
Set ISBN: 978-0-7166-0225-5

Printed in Malaysia by TWP Sdn Bhd, Johor Bahru
1st printing July 2011

Acknowledgments:
The publishers gratefully acknowledge the following sources for photography. All illustrations were prepared by
WORLD BOOK unless otherwise noted.

Cover: Corbis/Superstock; Shutterstock; NASA/ESA/H. E. Bond

B.A.E./Alamy Images 48; Buiten-Beeld/Alamy Images 23; Ethan Daniels, Alamy Images 22; Dreamstime 14,
17, 18, 24, 50; ESA 59; NASA 4, 5, 10, 26, 35, 37, 54, 58, 59; John Hill, Large Binocular Telescope Observatory
55; NASA/ESA, H. E. Bond 55; NASA/ESA/University of Arizona, Erich Karkoschka 40; NASA/Goddard
Space Flight Center 36; NASA/John Hopkins University Applied Physics Laboratory/Carnegie Institution of
Washington 34; NASA/JPL 41, 42; NASA/JPL-Caltech, R. Hurt 25; NASA/JPL/Space Science Institute 39,
43; NASA/JPL-Caltech/University of Arizona 42; NASA, Jack Pfaller 4; NASA/SDO/AIA 10; NASA/U.S.
Geological Survey 38; Sally Bensusen, Photo Researchers 23; © Larry Landolfi, Photo Researchers 49; Shutter-
stock 9, 19, 20, 21, 28, 56; UCO/Lick Observatory 30, 31.

Table of Contents

There is a glossary on page 62. Terms defined in the glossary are in type that **looks like this** on their first appearance on any spread (two facing pages).

What Is the Universe?

People have been watching the sky for thousands of years. They have seen light coming from shiny objects high in the sky. The sun shines in the daytime, the stars shine at night, and the moon sometimes glows day and night. These objects are far from Earth, the planet we live on. Earth and all the other planets and stars are part of one huge **universe.**

Powerful **telescopes** sent into space have taken pictures of many wonders, such as this group of stars.

← Galileo was a famous Italian astronomer. In 1609, Galileo used a telescope to view the moon. He was one of the first people to see the moon's surface in detail.

← Astronauts must wear special gear to protect their bodies in space.

The study of the stars, planets, and other heavenly bodies is called astronomy. It is one of the oldest sciences. **Astronomers** try to find out where these heavenly bodies are and how they move. They study what planets are made of. They learn about how stars create their light.

This book explores the sun, the moon, the planets, and the stars. In the pages that follow, you will find out what these heavenly bodies are made of and how scientists study them.

Rockets carry scientific equipment—and sometimes people—into space.

A Spinning World

Earth

Did you know that Earth is always moving? Earth is one of the eight planets that travel around the sun. Earth spins like a top. As it spins, it also moves through space.

Earth travels around the sun at a speed of about 66,700 miles (107,000 kilometers) an hour. But it isn't moving in a straight line. Instead, it whirls around the sun in a large, oval-shaped path. This path Earth takes around the sun is called an **orbit** (AWR biht).

What keeps Earth moving around the sun? Why doesn't it move all over space?

Everything in space pulls at everything else. This pull is called **gravity** (GRAV uh tee). The bigger an object is, the stronger its pull.

It takes about 365 days for Earth to complete one orbit around the sun.

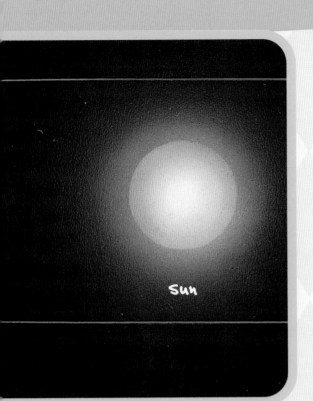

Sun

The sun is more than a million times bigger than Earth, so it tugs hard at Earth. It is this strong tug that keeps Earth in orbit.

The time it takes Earth to travel all the way around the sun is a little more than 365 days. This is what we call a year.

Try this!

Try this activity outside, a safe distance away from other people. Put a small rubber ball into the toe of an old, long sock. Hold the other end of the sock and whirl the ball around your head. Do you feel how the ball is trying to pull away? But you and the sock pull just as hard, like the pull that keeps Earth in the sun's orbit.

DRAW AN ORBIT

Try this activity to draw an **orbit**—the path of Earth or another planet around the sun.

MATERIALS

- Sheet of paper
- Board
- Piece of string
- Pencil
- 2 thumbtacks

DIRECTIONS

1. Place a sheet of paper on the board. Stick in the two thumbtacks so that they are about 4 to 5 inches (10 to 12.5 centimeters) apart.

2. Tie the ends of the string together and loop it around the thumbtacks. The loop should be 1 to 2 inches (2.5 to 5 centimeters) longer than the distance between the thumbtacks.

3. Place the pencil within the
   string, as shown below. Keeping
   the string tight, draw a line on
   the paper. Continue drawing all
   the way around the tacks.

You will find that you have drawn the shape of an oval. The
proper name for it is an ellipse. Planets orbit the sun or other
stars in ellipses. You can change the size and shape of the
ellipse by moving the tacks closer together or farther apart.

Planets in the **solar system** orbit
the sun in ellipses.

What Is the Sun?

The sun is a star. It is the closest star to Earth. The word *sun* comes from the word *Sol* (sahl). Sol was the name of the ancient Roman sun god. From the name *Sol* came the word *solar* (SOH luhr), which means "of the sun." The **solar system** includes everything that moves around the sun.

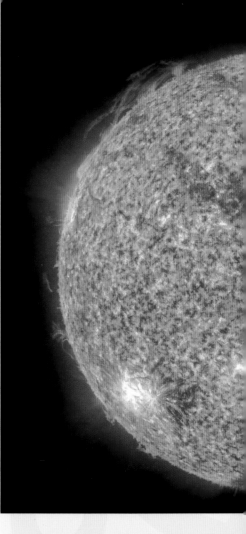

The sun is a glowing ball of extremely hot gases. ➜

The sun glows because it is extremely hot. The sun's center is a kind of giant furnace in which the temperature is about 27 million °F (15 million °C).

The sun may not look big from our view on Earth, but it is huge. At least 333,000 planets the size of Earth could fit into the sun! Why doesn't the sun look huge to us? The farther away something is, the smaller it appears. And the sun is about 93 million miles (150 million kilometers) from Earth.

The sun's surface is constantly churning. It sends erupting material out into space.

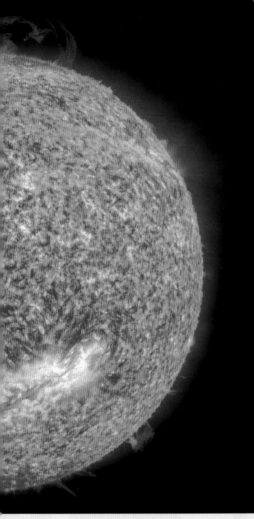

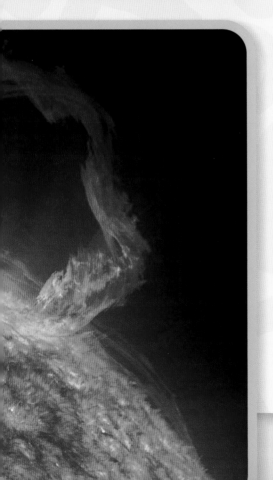

Without the sun, plants and animals could not survive. Energy comes up from inside the raging hot center of the sun. It reaches the sun's boiling, bubbling surface. Then it shoots out into space as light and heat. All living things must take in energy to stay alive. And nearly all energy comes from the sun. So the sun gives us much more than just light and heat. It truly gives us life.

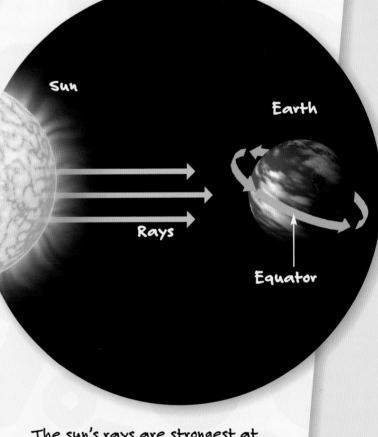

Sun

Earth

Rays

Equator

The sun's rays are strongest at the **equator** (an imaginary line around the middle of Earth). Regions near the equator are hot.

Activity

SCALING THE SUN

Try this activity outside in an open space. It will show you the scale of Earth and the sun in size and distance.

MATERIALS

- Sheets of cardboard
- Piece of string
- Drawing pin
- Pencil
- Ruler

DIRECTIONS

1. On a small sheet of cardboard, draw a circle about 0.25 inches (6 millimeters) across. This represents Earth.

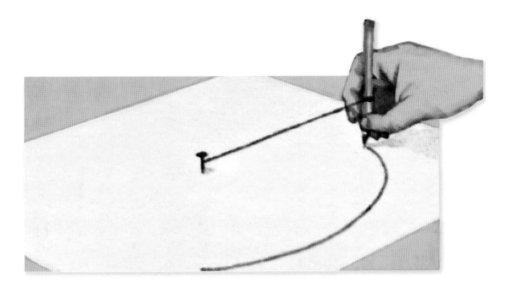

2. On a large sheet of cardboard, draw a circle 26 inches (66 centimeters) across. Do this by tying a pencil to a piece of string. Pin the other end of the string to the middle of the cardboard 13 inches (33 centimeters) away from the pencil. This represents the sun.

3. Take 150 steps to measure out a distance of about 250 feet (75 meters), and mark this place. Keep the Earth sheet yourself, and ask a friend to take the sun sheet and stand at the 250-foot mark.

The sun is much larger than Earth. The distance from the sun's center to its surface is about 109 times the distance from Earth's center to its surface. Even some of the streams of gas rising from the surface of the sun are larger than Earth!

250 feet

Why Does the Sun Disappear at Night?

The sun does not really disappear at night. It just seems to because the part of Earth you live on has turned away from it.

Earth is slowly spinning all the time. When it is morning, the part of Earth you live on is starting to face the sun. The sun seems low in the sky. As the day goes on, Earth continues to turn, and the sun appears higher in the sky. When your part of the world is most directly in line with the sun, it is the time of day we call noon.

No matter where you are on Earth, the sun rises in the east and sets in the west.

Day and Night Around the World

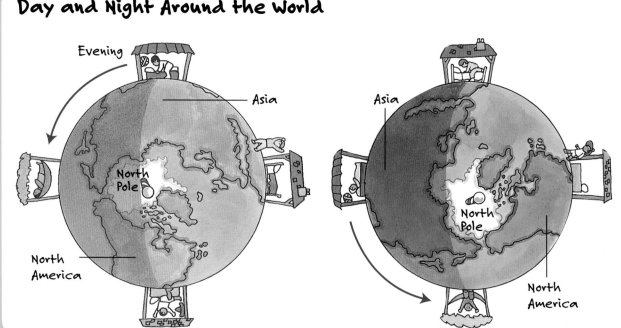

Evening

Asia

North Pole

North America

Asia

North Pole

North America

14

Slowly, your part of Earth moves away from the sun. That is why it gets darker and the sun seems to go down. Soon your part of Earth is completely away from the sun, and it is night.

At any time, half of Earth is getting light from the sun, while the other half is dark. As your part of Earth moves away from the sun, the other side is beginning to face the sun. There, the day is just beginning.

Try this!

Make a model Earth out of a round clay ball. Mark a small X on the ball to show the place where you live on Earth. Stick a pencil through the ball. In a dark room, shine a flashlight on your Earth. The flashlight will be the sun. Turn Earth slowly and watch what happens where you live. When is it daytime? When is it night? What if Earth didn't spin?

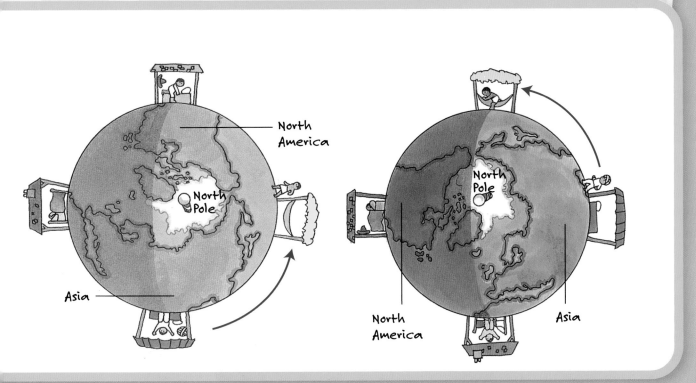

North America

North Pole

Asia

North Pole

North America

Asia

EYES ON THE SKIES

Have you ever wondered why the day sky is blue and the night sky is black? During daytime hours, when our side of Earth faces the sun, the sky is light. But during the night, when our side faces away from the sun, the sky is dark. When it's light, why is it blue rather than another color? Try the following experiment and find out.

DIRECTIONS

1. Place the clear glass filled with water at eye level in a darkened room.

2. Shine the flashlight at the glass of water so the beam of light goes through the center of the liquid.

3. Record what you see. Can you clearly see the beam of light pass through the water?

MATERIALS

- Clear glass filled with water
- Flashlight
- Whole milk
- Eyedropper
- Spoon
- Pen or pencil
- Paper or notebook

4. Now, using the eyedropper, place one drop of milk into the water. Stir the milk in the water with the spoon.

5. Take a moment to think about what may happen when you shine the light into the water. Record your prediction.

6. Now shine the flashlight into the water again. This time, what do you see? What do you think is causing the different color? How might the glass of milky water be like the sky? Record your observations and your explanation of what is happening. Can you explain what happened to the beam of light?

After you add the milk to the water, it should be a pale gray-blue. White light is made of different waves of color, and the waves are different sizes. When the light from the flashlight hits the tiny particles of milk mixed with the water, blue waves within the white light are separated and spread through the water, causing the water to look bluish. In the sky, particles of nitrogen and oxygen gas also separate blue light waves from the white sunlight, making the sky look blue.

Where's Your Shadow?

Take a walk outdoors early on a sunny morning, and your shadow will appear long. Later in the day, your shadow becomes short and almost seems to hide. Even later, just before sunset, your shadow will be long again. Why does your shadow grow and shrink while you stay exactly the same size?

Your shadow's size has to do with the sun's position in the sky. Every day, the sun appears to move across the sky. It rises in the east and sets in the west.

When the sun first comes up in the morning, it is very low in the sky. Most of your body blocks some light, so your shadow is very long. And since the sun always rises in the east, your morning shadow will always be to the west.

You see your shadow when your body blocks light. Your shadow shows as a dark patch because the light can't get through you.

Morning shadow

As the morning turns to noon, the sun gets higher in the sky, and your shadow becomes shorter. By noon, the sun forms a nearly straight line with your body. Your body is blocking very little light from the sun. This makes your shadow very short.

As afternoon passes, the sun's position continues to move across the sky. The sun moves downward, and your shadow grows long again, this time to the east. By the time the sun is ready to set in the evening, it is very low in the sky, and your shadow will once again be very long. As it gets dark, you can't make out your shadow anymore.

A sundial uses the position of a shadow to tell time.

Try this!

Find a sunny sidewalk with a friend. Make sure there are no trees or buildings that will block the sun during the day. Have your friend trace around your shadow in the morning, at noon, and late in the afternoon. Trace your friend's shadow, too. When are the shadows longest? When are they shortest?

Noon shadow

Evening shadow

What Are Seasons?

Summer comes to your part of the world when daylight begins early and stretches to almost bedtime or even later. The sunlight is also stronger. Winter comes when not as much of the sun's light reaches your part of the world.

Daylight hours are few in winter. It may be dark when you wake up, and dark when you get home from school. The ground and air cool off, too.

The difference in the amount of sunlight each season has is caused by the tilt of Earth. While Earth is spinning in space, it is also traveling around the sun. The planet's tilt causes the seasons as it travels around the sun.

Summer is the hottest season of the year.

Summer in the north

Winter in the south

Spring in the north

Fall in the south

Fall in the north

Spring in the south

Winter in the north

Summer in the south

The tilt of Earth's axis causes places to receive different amounts of sunlight during the year.

In some parts of the world, leaves change color during fall.

Many regions of the world have snowy winters.

As Earth moves, it spins like a top. It turns around an imaginary line called an **axis** (AK sihs). We think of this axis like a pole. We call one end the North Pole and we call the other end the South Pole.

Earth's axis is tilted, the way a top tilts when it is about to stop. When the North Pole is tilted toward the sun, the northern half of Earth gets more sunlight, and the southern half gets less sunlight. This makes it summer in the north and winter in the south.

Slowly, Earth moves around the sun. Soon the North Pole begins to tilt away from the sun. As this happens, the southern half tilts toward the sun. Then the northern half gets colder. It becomes fall, then winter, in the north. And the southern half gets warmer. It becomes spring, then summer, in the south.

During spring, plants begin to bloom.

An Eclipse of the Sun

It is the middle of the day. The sun hangs bright in the sky. Suddenly, the sky seems to be growing dark. The sun seems to be disappearing! Soon all you can see is what looks like a dark hole with a pale, fuzzy ring around it. What has happened?

During a solar eclipse, the sun appears to become dark as the moon passes between the sun and Earth.

The next time you are outdoors, look at a house in your neighborhood. Hold your hand in front of one eye so that you block your view of the house. Your hand is smaller than the house, but it is still blocking some of the house from your view. That is because the house is pretty far away. The farther away the house is, the more of it your hand can block. The moon, which is much smaller than the sun, can eclipse the sun in the same way.

22

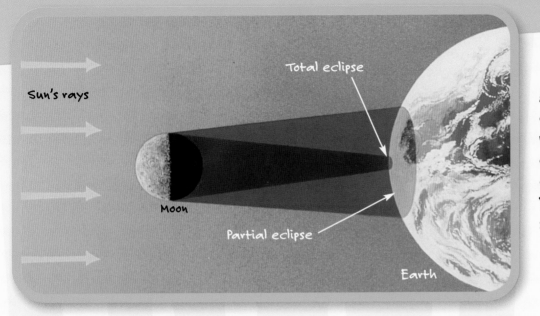

Sun's rays

Total eclipse

Moon

Partial eclipse

Earth

The moon, which moves around Earth, has passed between Earth and the sun. The sun is much bigger than the moon, but it is so far away from us that the moon seems to cover it up. When the moon is between the sun and Earth, the moon throws a shadow on Earth. The part of Earth covered by the shadow gets dark. This is a total **eclipse** (ih KLIHPS) of the sun, or a total solar eclipse.

Sometimes the moon covers only part of the sun. This is called a partial (PAHR shuhl) eclipse.

The sun's rays can hurt your eyes, so never look directly at the sun—even during an eclipse.

People must wear special glasses to protect their eyes when viewing a solar eclipse.

WARNING: Never stare directly at the sun. Even during an eclipse, the sun's direct rays can damage your eyes.

23

What Is the Moon?

The moon is the brightest object in the night sky. It is made of rock. The moon has no air and no liquid water. Most living things that we know of could not survive on the moon.

On some nights, the moon looks like a huge shining circle of light. On other nights, it looks like a thin, silver fingernail. But the moon does not really change its size or shape. And it does not make its own light. The light we see comes from the sun and bounces off the moon.

The stars are trillions of miles away. The sun is millions of miles away. But the moon is only about 239,000 miles (384,000 kilometers) away. As Earth moves through space, the moon is always beside it. The moon **orbits** Earth.

The moon is the brightest object in the night sky. The light we see comes from the sun and bounces off the moon.

The moon is smaller than most planets and stars. If Earth were the size of a basketball, the moon would be about the size of a tennis ball.

Long ago, many groups of people worshiped the moon. The ancient Romans named the moon Luna. The word *lunar* (LOO nuhr) means "of the moon."

Try this!

On a clear night, especially a night when the moon is full or almost full, look carefully to see what shapes you can find on the moon's surface. If you have binoculars, use them. Use your imagination. What do you see? Can you see "the man in the moon"?

The moon moves in an almost circular path around Earth. This path is called an orbit.

What Is the Moon Like?

The moon has many large craters. Some craters formed when meteoroids crashed into the moon.

The surface of the moon is not the same all over. In some areas, it has broad, flat plains covered with powdery rock dust. In other areas, it has rugged mountains. It also has billions of round holes in the ground called **craters** (KRAY tuhrs).

An astronaut's footprints are left on the moon's powdery surface. Astronauts first set foot on the moon in 1969.

Some of the craters are no bigger than a pencil point. Some are the size of a car tire. And some are bigger than the Grand Canyon! The biggest crater on the moon is more than 700 miles (1,100 kilometers) across.

What formed the moon's craters and mountains? Chunks of rock called **meteoroids** (MEE tee uh royds) move around the sun, just as Earth and the moon do. Sometimes these meteoroids crash into the moon. The moon and the meteoroids move so fast that the meteoroids make craters in the moon's surface when they crash.

When meteoroids strike, they usually form walls of rock around the craters they make. Many of the moon's mountains are really walls made by meteoroids.

MAKE YOUR OWN CRATERS

You can create your own craters by following these simple steps.

MATERIALS

- Newspapers
- Plastic trash bag
- Baking pan or dishpan
- 4-5 cupfuls of dry clay
- Water
- Several rocks, a variety of shapes and sizes
- Ruler
- Paper
- Pen or pencil

DIRECTIONS

1. Cover your work area with newspapers. Slip the trash bag over the pan to line it. In the pan, mix the clay with water. Make it soft enough to mold easily.

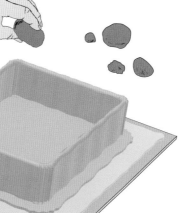

2. The rocks are your "meteoroids." Drop them into the box, one at a time, from different heights. To make some of them hit at different angles, tip the box.

Meteoroid One
- 2 in. x 5 in.
- Depth of 1/4 in.
- Drop 2 in. high

Note each meteoroid's size and shape and the height and angle from which you drop it. Also note how your "moon" looks. Measure the depth and shape of each crater. Sketch your "moon" with craters.

Why Does the Moon Change Shape?

The moon seems to change from a thin crescent to a full circle. Each time the moon looks different, we say it is in a new phase. A **phase** is a change in the moon's shape as it is seen from Earth.

In the phase known as "new moon," the moon cannot be seen at all because it is between Earth and the sun. The sun is shining on the side of the moon that faces the sun, but there is no sunlight on the side that faces us. All we see is darkness.

After a day or two, the moon will seem to have moved slightly away from the sun. Then we can see a tiny bit of the side that is sunlit. We call this phase a crescent moon.

The shape of the moon appears to change as the moon travels around Earth.

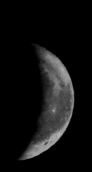
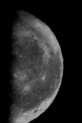

Waxing gibbous moon

Waxing half moon

Waxing crescent moon

The moon looks like a crescent shape when only a small part of its sunlit side is turned toward Earth.

After about seven days, we can see half of the moon's sunlit side. This phase is called a half moon.

After about two weeks, the moon is halfway around Earth from where it started. Now we can see the whole side of the moon that the sun is shining on. We call this phase a full moon. The moon keeps moving, and the part we can see gets smaller and smaller. Finally, the moon is between Earth and the sun again.

Sometimes Earth comes between the moon and the sun. This event is called a lunar **eclipse.** In a lunar eclipse, a dark shadow falls across the face of the moon. This is the shadow of Earth.

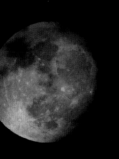
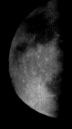
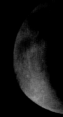

Full moon

Waning gibbous moon

Waning half moon

Waning crescent moon

PHASES OF THE MOON

Why does the moon have **phases**? See for yourself by doing this experiment.

DIRECTIONS

MATERIALS
- Flashlight
- Dark-colored ball

1. Place the flashlight on a table or shelf. Set the ball on a surface of the same height. Then shine the light on it. The flashlight acts as the sun. The ball is the moon. You are the planet Earth.

2. Sit directly between the light and the front of the ball, but beneath the beam of light. The whole side of the ball facing you will be in light, like a full moon is.

Full moon

3. Move to the "side" of the ball. You will see half of the ball in the light, like a half moon.

Half moon

4. Move around the ball a little more, so that the ball is nearly between you and the light. Most of the ball will be in shadow. Only a small part will be in the light, like a crescent moon.

Crescent moon

Now you know why the moon has different phases. The moon and Earth change positions in relation to the sun.

Sun

Mercury

Earth

Venus

Mars

Asteroid Belt

Jupiter

Saturn

What Is the Solar System?

The **solar system** contains the sun and the many objects that travel around it. Some are planets much larger than Earth. Others are tiny **meteoroids** and bits of dust.

There are eight planets in the solar system. Each of them moves around the sun in a certain path called an **orbit.**

Two planets, Mercury and Venus, are very close to the sun. The others are much farther away. Two planets in the solar system are smaller than Earth. One is about the same size. And four are much bigger.

Like Earth and the moon, the other planets in the solar system reflect the sun's light. That's why we can see some of them at night.

Uranus

Neptune

Kuiper Belt begins

*Distances are not proportional.

Try this!

The solar system includes the sun and planets and other objects orbiting around it. This illustration shows how big the planets are in relation to one another.

Use words that begin with the letters m, v, e, m, j, s, u, and n—in that order—to form a fun sentence. Memorize the sentence. When you need to remember the planets in order, just think of your sentence and the first letter of each word. Here is an example: My Very Excited Mother Just Sang Until Noon. Now you try!

Mercury

Mercury is the planet closest to the sun. It is a bare rocky ball covered with **craters,** much like our moon. Also like our moon, Mercury has broad, flat plains and steep cliffs.

Mercury spins and has day and night, but it spins very slowly. One day on Mercury takes 59 Earth days.

Mercury is very hot during the day. Temperatures there reach higher than 800 °F (420 °C). At night, temperatures take a big dip, sometimes to nearly −280 °F (−170 °C)!

Before beginning its **orbit** around Mercury, the Messenger spacecraft flew by the planet twice in 2008. It photographed areas of its surface that had never been seen before.

Mercury has bigger changes of temperature than any other planet. This is because it is closest to the sun, and because it has very long days.

Mercury is a small planet. Earth is 2 ½ times as wide across as Mercury. There are hardly any gases surrounding Mercury, so it has very little **atmosphere** (all gases that surround a planet).

People could not live on Mercury because it is too hot during the day and too cold at night. But scientists have explored it with a spacecraft that had no people aboard.

Venus

Venus is nearly the same size as Earth, so it is often called Earth's "twin." But its surface is nothing like Earth's. Venus has an atmosphere full of poisonous gases. Its clouds contain a chemical strong enough to dissolve metal! And the clouds on Venus are so thick that cameras can't see the planet's surface.

Powerful windstorms rage high in Venus's atmosphere. These windstorms are much worse than storms on Earth. Lightning flashes in the sky as often as 20 times a minute.

Venus is the second closest planet to the sun. It is extremely hot and dry. As seen from Earth, Venus is brighter than all the other planets and stars. It is so bright that it can sometimes be seen from Earth in the daytime! A year on Venus is as long as 225 Earth days.

This computer image of Venus's surface shows how it might appear under its layer of thick clouds.

Earth

Earth is a watery
planet. More than
two-thirds of Earth's
surface is covered with
water. That's good for all the
living things in our world because
animals and plants need water to live.
Animals and plants live almost everywhere on Earth.

Earth is the third planet from the sun. Its
atmosphere is made up of nitrogen, oxygen, and
carbon dioxide. These gases are needed for almost all
living things to survive. Animals breathe in oxygen.
Plants need carbon dioxide.

Earth travels 595 million miles (958 million
kilometers) around the sun. It takes about 365 days for
Earth to **orbit** the sun once. That's why there are
about 365 days in an Earth year.

Earth is the only
watery planet in the
solar system.

Mars

Mars is the fourth planet from the sun. It is known as the red planet because it has a reddish tint. What makes Mars red? Its dry, desertlike regions are covered by rust-colored dust, sand, and rocks. Windstorms whirl the orange-colored sand up from the plains and fill the air with dust. This dust gives the Martian sky a reddish color as well.

There are many canyons, **craters,** and volcanoes on Mars. One volcano, called Olympus Mons, is nearly three times as high as Mount Everest, the highest mountain on Earth. In fact, Olympus Mons is the largest volcano in the entire **solar system!**

Mars is about half as wide across as Earth.

In 2003, the Hubble Space Telescope took this image of Mars.

Jupiter

Jupiter is the biggest planet in the **solar system.** It would take more than 1,000 Earths to fill up Jupiter!

Jupiter is the fifth planet from the sun. Scientists think it may have a small, rocky core (center), but most of it is surrounded by liquid and thick clouds of gas. The clouds form colored bands around the planet. Jupiter also has three thin rings of dust that sometimes look like one.

Jupiter's surface is made of thick red, brown, yellow, and white clouds. The Great Red Spot can be seen in the lower left side of this image.

Wild windstorms are always raging in Jupiter's thick clouds. Can you imagine a huge hurricane that whirls for 300 years? Scientists believe that a hurricane on Jupiter called the Great Red Spot has been whirling for at least that long. This hurricane is more than three times as wide as Earth!

Scientists have sent **space probes** (rockets with scientific instruments) to study Jupiter. From 1995 to 2003, the U.S. spacecraft Galileo **orbited** Jupiter. In 2003, Galileo was sent crashing into Jupiter's **atmosphere.**

Saturn

Saturn, the sixth planet from the sun, is famous for its set of gleaming rings. Saturn has seven major rings and many ringlets.

Saturn's rings are made of billions of pieces of ice and rock, from tiny specks to very large "moonlets." These bits of ice and rock travel around Saturn just as the moon orbits Earth.

Saturn is the second largest planet. It probably has a rocky center, which may be covered by a thin layer of liquid. And it is surrounded by thick layers of gas.

Scientists used the space probes Voyager 1 and Voyager 2 to study Saturn. Launched in 1997, the U.S. spacecraft Cassini was sent to explore Saturn's rings and its moons. Soon after its arrival, Cassini launched a probe named Huygens to the surface of Saturn's largest moon, Titan, in 2005.

Saturn has seven thin, flat rings made of small pieces of ice.

Uranus

In 1781, a British **astronomer** named William Herschel looked through a homemade **telescope,** an object that helps us see things that are too far away to be seen with our eyes alone. Herschel found a new planet, Uranus, which became the first planet to be discovered without the eyes alone.

Uranus is the seventh planet from the sun. It is a blue-green planet nearly four times as wide as Earth. Scientists believe that Uranus has a rocky core covered by a deep ocean and thick clouds of gas. Uranus has at least 13 thin rings.

When Earth spins on its **axis,** it is tilted like a spinning top. But the axis of Uranus is tilted more than any other planet. At times, Uranus's north pole is pointed almost straight toward the sun. About 42 Earth years later, it is pointed away from the sun. Scientists learned much about Uranus from the **space probe** Voyager 2, which flew past the planet in 1986.

Uranus is surrounded by faint rings and at least 27 moons.

Neptune

Neptune is the farthest planet from the sun. It is the only planet that cannot be seen without a telescope. Neptune is about 30 times farther from the sun than Earth. It **orbits** the sun about once every 165 Earth years.

Neptune is about the same size as Uranus and is also about four times as wide across as Earth. The planet is mostly made up of gases, but Neptune's center may be a mixture of slush and rocks.

Neptune is surrounded by thick layers of clouds in rapid motion. Winds blow these clouds at speeds up to about 1,250 miles (2,000 kilometers) per hour. The planet has four faint rings that scientists think are made of dust. It has at least 13 moons.

A dark spot on Neptune, seen at the center of this image, is made up of swirling masses of gas resembling a hurricane. This area is called the Great Dark Spot.

Jupiter (upper right) has four planet-sized moons.

The Moons of Other Planets

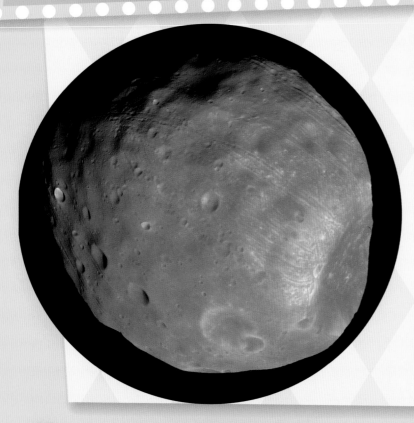

Earth is not the only planet that has a moon. Other planets do, too!

Mars has two little moons that are lumpy chunks of rock. The largest, Phobos, is only about 17 miles (27 kilometers) wide. Mars's other moon, Deimos, is about 9 miles (15 kilometers) wide.

Phobos is Mars's largest moon. Many scientists believe that it is an asteroid (rocky object) that was "captured" by Mars's gravity.

Jupiter has at least 63 moons. A few of the smallest moons are smaller than some of the mountains on Earth. But the biggest, Ganymede, is bigger than the planet Mercury.

Saturn has at least 62 moons. Like Jupiter's moons, Saturn's are very different in size. About a dozen are less than 25 miles (40 kilometers) across. But the biggest moon, Titan, is bigger than Earth's moon. Titan is also bigger than Mercury.

Before 1989, it was thought that Neptune had only two moons. But that year, the U.S. **space probe** Voyager 2 flew past Neptune and discovered six smaller, dark moons. In 2002 and 2003, five additional moons were discovered, bringing the total to 13.

Iapetus is one of Saturn's many moons.

Try this!

Some scientists think that Jupiter's moon Europa and Saturn's moon Titan may be able to support life. Research one of these moons and find out what it's made of. Imagine what kind of creature might be able to live on this moon. Draw a picture of your creature and write down how each of its features might help it to survive in its environment.

MAKE A SPACE MOBILE

Make a model of the **solar system** like the one below. Ask an adult to help you with this activity.

DIRECTIONS

1. Cross the two longer dowel rods so one end of each rod sticks out 1 inch (2.5 centimeters) farther than the other end, as shown below. Tie them together with nylon thread. Do the same with the two shorter rods. Tie a ring above and below each pair of rods at the points where the rods cross.

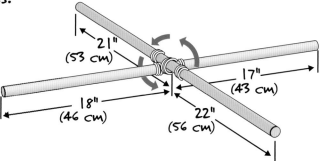

21"
(53 cm)

17"
(43 cm)

18"
(46 cm)

22"
(56 cm)

2. Cut an 8-inch (20-centimeter) piece of nylon thread. Tie one end of the thread to the ring below the longer rods and the other end to the ring on top of the shorter rods. Leave 6 inches (15 centimeters) of thread between the rings.

3. Cut one 32-inch (81-centimeter) piece of thread and nine 16-inch (41-centimeter) pieces of thread. Tie the longer thread to the ring on top of the longer rods. Tie one of the shorter threads to the ring below the shorter rods. Hang the mobile from the longer thread on a hook. Then tie one thread to the end of each rod. Tie a second thread to the longer side of the longest rod.

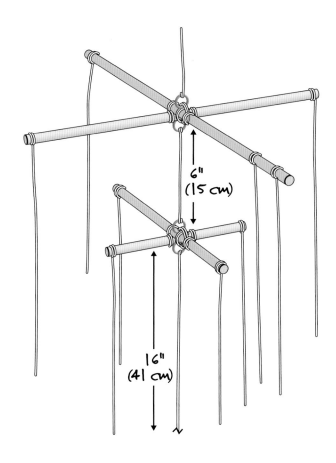

MATERIALS

- 4 dowel rods:
  one 17 inches (43 centimeters)
  one 21 inches (53 centimeters)
  one 35 inches (89 centimeters)
  one 43 inches (109 centimeters)

- Spool of clear nylon thread or fishing line

- 4 plastic or metal rings, ³/₄ inch (2 centimeters) across

- Large piece of white poster board

- Geometric compass

- Scissors

- Glue

- Crayons or markers

- Tape

- Hole punch

- Yardstick

- Large paper plate

- Small hook for hanging the mobile

MAKE A SPACE MOBILE

Activity continued

4. To make the planets and the sun, draw nine circles on the poster board using a geometric compass. Set your compass to the radii (distances from the center) shown in the chart below. Ask an adult to help you if you don't know how to use a compass.

SUN:	4 1/2 inches (11.5 centimeters)
JUPITER:	3 3/4 inches (9.5 centimeters)
SATURN:	3 1/4 inches (8.5 centimeters)
NEPTUNE:	2 1/2 inches (6.5 centimeters)
URANUS:	2 1/4 inches (6 centimeters)
EARTH:	1 1/2 inches (4 centimeters)
VENUS:	1 1/4 inches (3.5 centimeters)
MARS:	1 1/8 inches (3 centimeters)
MERCURY:	1 inch (2.5 centimeters)

5. Color both sides of your sun and planets. Use pictures of planets from pages 30-39 of this book to guide you, or find other pictures of the planets to use.

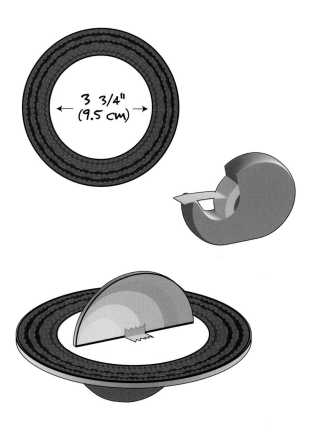

6. Use the paper plate for Saturn's ring. Color just the outer edge of the plate, as shown to the right. Cut a slit about 3 ³/₄ inches (9.5 centimeters) long in the middle of the plate. Slip the Saturn model through the slit and tape it in place.

7. Punch a hole near the top of your sun and each planet. Tie your sun and planets to the mobile, as shown to the right. Mercury, the planet closest to the sun, should hang from the shortest section of rod, Venus from the next shortest section, and so on, in each planet's order from the sun. Uranus and Neptune should hang from the longest rod. Look at the picture of the finished mobile on page 42 for help. Now you can hang the **solar system** anywhere you like!

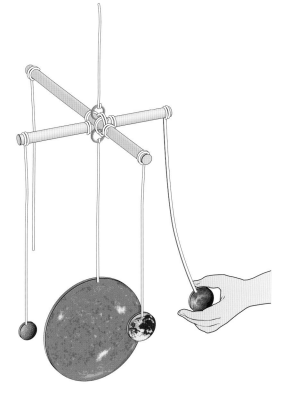

The Milky Way is a huge group of stars and other objects in space. On clear, dark nights, it appears as a broad, milky-looking band of starlight stretching across the sky.

What Are Stars?

In addition to the planets, there are countless stars in the **universe.** Stars are huge balls of glowing gas in the sky. The sun is the only star close enough to Earth to look like a large ball to us. The other stars are so far away that they look like tiny dots of light.

Stars may look close, but they are actually very far away—much farther from Earth than the planets are. The nearest star to us, after the sun, is so far away that it takes more than four years for its light to reach us! Some stars are so far away that their light takes billions of years to reach us.

How many stars are there? Scientists believe that there are about 10 billion trillion stars in the universe. To understand how large a number this is, imagine that all the people in the world had to count an equal number of stars one by one. Each person would have to count more than 1 ½ trillion stars. And, even if you could count 1,000 stars per second for 24 hours a day, you would need 50 years to count 1 ½ trillion stars!

Where do stars go during the day? They don't go anywhere. The sun makes our daytime sky so bright that we can't see any other stars.

This photograph, taken over an eight-hour period, shows the movement of the stars across the sky.

Star Pictures

If you look up at the sky at night, you might imagine pictures or shapes in the stars. Long ago, people used their imaginations to find star pictures, too. People named star groups after the pictures they made.

Today, some people still use these star pictures, called **constellations,** to find the stars they want to study.

This chart shows constellations and bright stars you can see in the Northern Hemisphere.

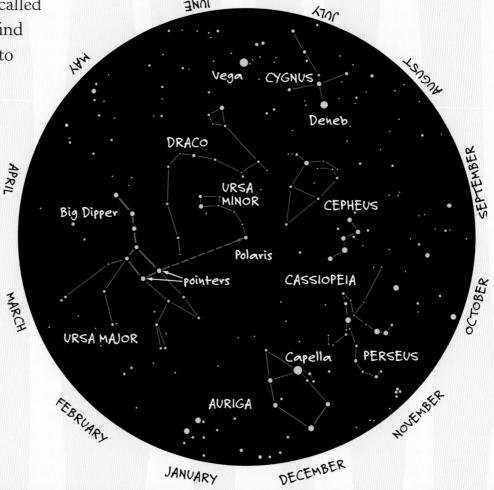

If you live in the Northern Hemisphere, you will be able to see the constellations shown on the star chart on page 50 during most of the year. If you live in the Southern Hemisphere, you will be able to see the constellations shown on the star chart on page 51 during most of the year. And if you live in the southern United States, Hawaii, northern Australia, or somewhere close to the **equator,** you will sometimes be able to see some of the constellations on both charts.

On the charts, stars in each constellation are joined with lines that show the constellation's shape. Each constellation has a Latin name. Some of the names are based on what ancient people thought the constellations looked like.

The constellation Orion includes two of the brightest stars in the sky.

If you live in or near a city, you may not be able to see all of the stars or constellations because of the city lights. But you will almost always be able to see the brightest stars on cloudless nights.

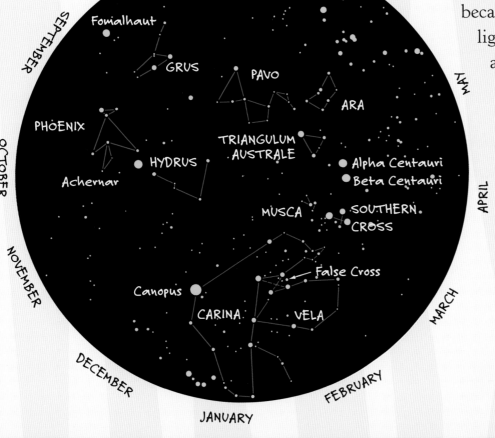

One of the most famous constellations in the Southern Hemisphere is the Southern Cross.

PLANETARIUM AT HOME

Try this activity to make your own model of the night sky. In a planetarium, light is used to form patterns on walls, ceilings, or other surfaces. With your planetarium, you can stargaze during the day and on rainy nights.

MATERIALS

- Round oatmeal container with lid
- Scissors
- Pen
- Tracing paper
- Black construction paper
- Different-sized paper punches
- Pencil
- Flashlight

DIRECTIONS

1. Cut out the bottom of the oatmeal box and the center of the lid.

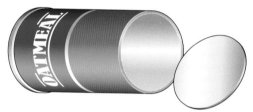

2. Cut the center out of the lid, leaving at least a half-inch (1.27-centimeter) space at the edge.

3. Using the tracing paper, trace the dots in the **constellation** on this page.

4. Trace the outside of the box lid on the construction paper. Cut out the circle. Trim it just inside the line, so that it fits inside the lid.

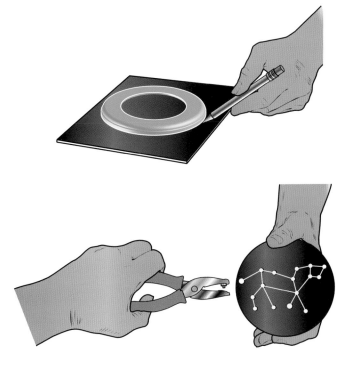

5. Place the tracing of the constellation over the tracing of the lid. Use the large, medium, and small punches to make different-sized holes for stars. Or punch the holes with a pencil, making the ones for brighter stars larger.

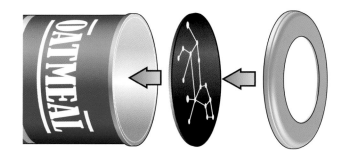

6. Fit the circle of construction paper inside the lid. Place the lid on the box.

7. Go into a completely dark room. Put the flashlight into the box from the bottom, and turn it on. Look up. You should see the constellation on the ceiling.

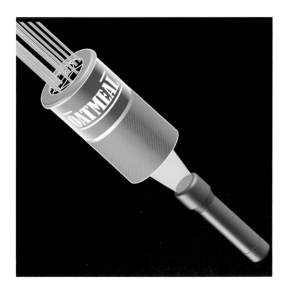

8. Find constellations in books and trace them. Then make more construction paper circles, and punch the constellations into them.

Observing the Night Sky

Since ancient times, people have studied heavenly bodies. **Astronomers** of the past knew only about the objects they could see with just their eyes or with basic **telescopes.** Today, astronomers have powerful telescopes, computers, and many other tools to help them learn about the **universe.**

Observatories are like houses for telescopes. Some observatories have cameras and other machines that record the information gathered by telescopes. Most observatories are easy to spot. Many of them have a dome that looks like an upside-down bowl. The dome keeps the telescope safe from bad weather.

The Large Binocular Telescope is an observatory on Mount Graham in Arizona. It is built like a giant pair of binoculars. →

The James Webb Space Telescope is scheduled to launch around 2014-2015. Scientists hope that the powerful telescope will capture images of distant parts of the universe.

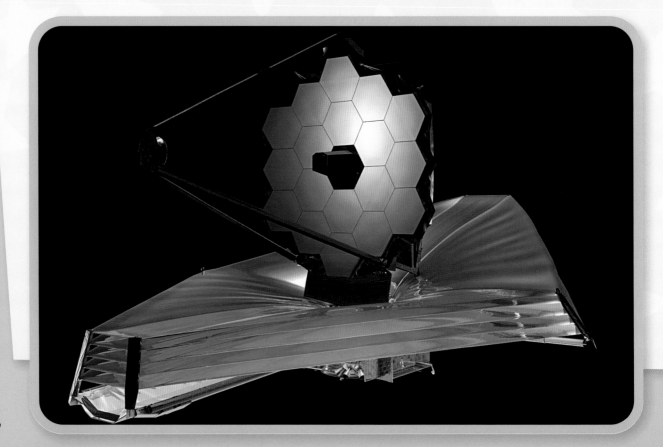

Scientists have also launched telescopes into space to observe heavenly bodies. The Hubble Space Telescope is a powerful **orbiting** telescope that provides sharper images of heavenly bodies than other telescopes do.

Scientists first launched the Hubble telescope into space in 1990. Astronomers have used it to obtain images of heavenly bodies in detail never before observed. These include pictures of stars surrounded by dusty disks that might someday become new stars and planets. Hubble has also captured images of galaxies (systems of stars, gases, and dust) on the edge of the observable universe.

The Hubble Space Telescope has taken spectacular images of heavenly bodies, such as this supergiant star and a cloud of gas that surrounds it.

TABLETOP TELESCOPE

Try this activity to make a simple **telescope** you can use to observe the night sky.

DIRECTIONS

1. Place the magnifying mirror near a window to reflect the moon or stars. The mirror should stand at an angle to the window so the light will be reflected to another surface.

2. Prop up the flat mirror so light from the magnifying mirror will be reflected off it. From behind the magnifying mirror, you should see light reflected from the moon or the stars in the flat mirror. You may need to adjust the position of both mirrors to get a good reflection of the moon or a group of stars. Every few minutes you will have to readjust the mirrors if you want to track the motion of the moon and stars.

3. Use your magnifying glass to examine the reflection that appears in the flat mirror. Move the magnifying glass back and forth until you see the reflection clearly.

How well your telescope works depends on the quality of your magnifying glass and on finding the right distance and positions between the mirrors.

Exploring the Universe

One of the greatest adventures in history took place on July 20, 1969. Two astronauts, Neil Armstrong and Buzz Aldrin, set foot on the moon. They had traveled nearly 240,000 miles (386,000 kilometers) across space.

Since that time, many other scientists have traveled into space. From 1981 to 2011, they traveled in space shuttles. A space shuttle is powered by rocket booster motors and powerful engines. Scientists are currently developing new spacecraft that may travel to the moon and Mars.

Buzz Aldrin was one of two astronauts to first set foot on the moon.

The International Space Station functions as an observatory, laboratory, and workshop.

Some people have lived in space for periods of time. A space station is a place where scientists and technicians can live and work in space for weeks or months. Space stations are very large. Smaller spacecraft are used to carry people between Earth and the space station. Other spacecraft are used to supply the station with food, water, equipment, and mail.

Scientists have also sent **space probes** to explore the **universe.** A space probe is a spacecraft with no people on board. A probe may go far out into space, or it may land on a planet or moon. Some space probes bring samples back to Earth. Others make one-way journeys, sending back photographs and information.

This illustration shows the Huygens probe landing on the surface of Titan, Saturn's largest moon.

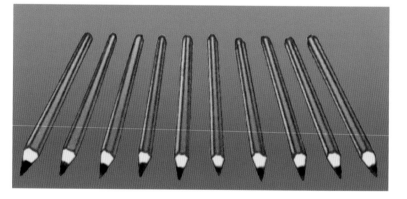

MAKE ROCKET FUEL

Spacecraft need rockets to launch them into space. See how rocket fuel works with this activity. This experiment makes a mess, so it is best to do it outside!

MATERIALS

- Small plastic bottle
- Cork
- 10 pencils
- Baking powder
- Teaspoon
- Water

DIRECTIONS

1. Place 10 pencils side by side, about 1 inch (2.5 centimeters) apart.

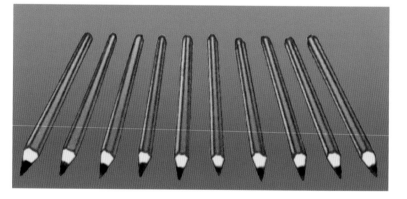

2. Put about five heaping teaspoons of baking powder inside the bottle. Now pour enough water into the bottle to cover the baking powder.

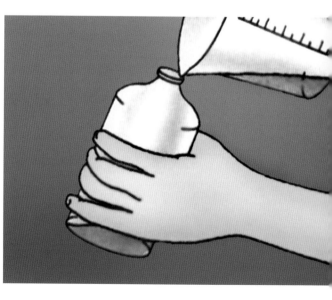

3. Ask an adult to quickly place the cork in the bottle and place the bottle on the pencils. Do not put the cork in too tightly. Quickly move far back from and to one side of the bottle.

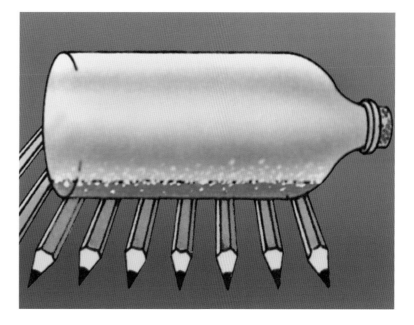

The baking powder and water will start fizzing and making lots of gas. Pressure builds up inside and soon forces out the cork. As the cork shoots out, the bottle shoots in the opposite direction over the pencils.

Glossary

astronomer a person who studies the planets, stars, sun, moon, and other heavenly bodies.

atmosphere all gases that surround Earth or any other planet.

axis an imaginary line through an object, around which the object turns.

constellation a group of stars that seems to take on a special shape as viewed from Earth.

crater a bowl-shaped hole on the surface of a planet, moon, or other solid body.

eclipse the blocking of light from the sun or the moon.

equator an imaginary line that circles the middle of Earth. It is halfway between the North Pole and the South Pole.

gravity a natural force that draws things toward Earth's surface or toward each other.

meteoroid a chunk of metal or stone that rushes through outer space. When it enters Earth's atmosphere, it burns up, leaving a trail of glowing gas. We call this trail a meteor or shooting star.

orbit (n.) the path that a planet or other object follows as it circles another body; (v.) to travel around a planet or other object.

solar system the sun, the planets, and all other heavenly bodies that orbit the sun.

space probe a spacecraft that carries scientific instruments to make observations in space and send the information back to Earth.

telescope an instrument for making distant objects appear nearer and larger.

universe everything that exists, including Earth, the stars, planets, and other heavenly bodies.

Find Out More

Books

Children's Night Sky Atlas by Robin Scagell (DK Publishing, 2004)

Destination, Space by Seymour Simon (HarperCollins Publishers, 2002)

Far-Out Science Projects about Earth's Sun and Moon by Robert Gardner and Tom LaBaff (Enslow Publishers, 2008)

Moon by Steve Tomecek and Lisa Chauncy Guida (National Geographic Society, 2005)

Planets! by Lisa Jo Rudy (HarperCollins Publishers, 2005)

Stars by Steve Tomecek and Sachiko Yoshikawa (National Geographic, 2003)

Websites

BBC's The Solar System
http://www.bbc.co.uk/science/space/solarsystem/sun_and_planets/sun
Tour the solar system at this educational website from the British Broadcasting Corporation.

Dawn: A Journey to the Beginning of the Solar System
http://dawn.jpl.nasa.gov/DawnKids/
Follow along with NASA's Dawn mission as it explores the asteroid belts in search of clues about the beginning of our solar system.

Dome of the Sky
http://domeofthesky.com/foyer.html
Learn about the constellations and the myths behind them at this virtual observatory.

Kids Astronomy
http://www.kidsastronomy.com/
At this website, you can explore deep space, track the phases of the moon, and map the positions of the stars.

Marc's Observatory
http://www.marcsobservatory.com/
At this interactive website, you can track the phases of the moon, learn fun facts about stars and constellations, and learn to use a star chart, among other activities.

NASA Kids' Club
http://www.nasa.gov/audience/forkids/kidsclub/flash/index.html
At this educational website, you can read about NASA's latest missions and meet the scientists and astronauts who are working to explore our solar system.

StarChild
http://starchild.gsfc.nasa.gov/docs/starchild/StarChild.html
This learning center for young astronomers is maintained by the U.S. National Aeronautics and Space Administration (NASA).

Views of the Solar System
http://www.solarviews.com/
Pictures, videos, and animations paint a vivid picture of our solar system at this website.

Index

Activities